SUFFOLK
SMUGGLERS' PUBS

Terry Townsend

To my wife Carol
for in every sense this is her book, too

ACKNOWLEDGEMENTS

Thanks also to Adrienne Bradney-Smith
and Brenda and Tony Stables
for their continued help and support

First published in Great Britain in 2017

Copyright © Terry Townsend 2017

British Library Cataloguing-in-Publication Data
A CIP record for this title is available from the
British Library

ISBN 978 0 85710 114 3

PiXZ Books
Halsgrove House, Ryelands Business Park,
Bagley Road, Wellington, Somerset TA21 9PZ
Tel: 01823 653777
Fax: 01823 216796
email: sales@halsgrove.com

An imprint of Halstar Ltd, part of the
Halsgrove group of companies
Information on all Halsgrove titles is
available at: www.halsgrove.com

Printed and bound in India by
Parksons Graphics

CONTENTS

A SHIP HAS BEEN SIGHTED
in this quarter
ENGAGING IN THE UNLAWFUL ACT OF

SMUGGLING

whosoever can lay information
leading to the capture of this ship
or its crew

will receive a reward of

£500

From His Majesty's Government

This 19th day of October 1782

Introduction

Smuggling in Suffolk

By 1700, when Britain had become a military and sea power to be reckoned with, the government was obliged to meet the ever-increasing expense of defending its interests. Britain was now waging war in some part of the world well-nigh continuously. By the mid-eighteenth century, war with foreign powers had become an accepted way of life. To fund the conflicts successive governments imposed taxes on the importation of a large range of luxury goods and in doing so the law makers unwittingly created a climate for smuggling.

By 1760 the list of luxuries subject to customs import tax had grown to 800, and over the next fifty years another 1300 items were added. Despite political disagreements and military conflicts merchants on the continent had no qualms in making tax-free goods available to any English entrepreneurs with money to pay for them.

Purchasing tax-free goods from Holland and France and selling to an eager home market was a very profitable, if somewhat dangerous pastime. 'Free Trading' as it became known to those involved, was the inevitable result of punitive taxation. In Suffolk, as in other coastal counties, it quickly developed into a massive crime wave.

During the eighteenth century vast quantities of contraband were landed on Suffolk's open beaches.

On Monday, 4 February 1734, Walter Plummer MP told the House of

5

Commons he had recently been in Suffolk where smugglers went about in such formidable bodies, that if something was not done to put a stop to them: *'they might soon threaten danger even to the Government'*. He went on to say he had often met them in gangs of forty or fifty together, all so well mounted, that even the Dragoons *'could not come up with them'*.

The Honourable Member struck at the root of the problem when he outlined the economics. During the mid-eighteenth century the average wage for a Suffolk farm hand was eighteen pence a day. In Plummer's opinion this was apparently good because he said: *'Even at that price it is with great difficulty that the farmers can get labourers, and how can it be otherwise?'*

Sailing cutters packed with contraband regularly arrived from the continent and anchored a couple of miles off the Suffolk shore. A flotilla of rowing boats and shallow draught luggers capable of beach landings, rendezvoused with the larger ships and crews transferred the goods.

The smuggling gang masters paid half-a-crown a day to men who waited on the beaches and helped with unloading. Other men who transferred the goods onto

Smuggling gang masters paid half-a-crown a day to beach crew men who: *'were well entertained during their attendance'*.

horses and into carts were paid up to ten times more if they helped deliver luxury items to customers across the county and beyond. Both teams: *'were well entertained during their attendance'.*

The consequence, Plummer explained was: '... *all the young clever fellows of the county are employed by the smugglers. The smugglers gave such excessive wages to the men that would engage with them, that landed interest suffered considerably by it... Thus they find a much easier and more profitable employment than they can have from the farmer, and while they are thus employed all improvements of the land must remain in suspense.'*

The MP sadly concluded: *'whatever methods might be adopted with the aim of stamping out smuggling must all prove inefficient as long as duty was so high and so much advantage was to be got from running'.* He was proved right and in spite of attempts at suppressing the free trade it continued virtually unabated throughout the eighteenth century which became known as smuggling's 'golden age'.

Gin, Tea, Brandy and Tobacco

Of the hundreds of luxury items subject to customs duty, Suffolk smugglers were mainly involved in the illegal importation of gin, tea, brandy and tobacco. Gin came from the Dutch distilleries in the city of Schiedam west of Rotterdam. It was known at the time as 'Hollands' or 'Geneva' from the Dutch word for juniper used to flavour the pure spirit. Schiedam, whose main industry was the production of gin, earned the nickname 'Black Nazareth' for the palls of sooty smoke belching from dozens of distillery chimneys.

Dutch merchants who shipped gin also became involved in supplying tea they bought at sixpence a pound in the Dutch East Indies and sold to Suffolk smugglers for two shillings a pound, less than half the price of the imposed duty.

Brandy and tobacco came mainly from Northern France. Seizing the opportunity, some Suffolk merchants set up supply warehouses at Dunkirk and Calais alongside French enterprises.

The Scale of the Problem

No Suffolk smugglers' records have been found to date. However, customs' reports make clear the enormous scale of the problem. *The Victoria History of Suffolk* states it was estimated in the second half of 1745 alone, 3524 horse-loads of contraband were run into Suffolk and of that amount, 1835 loads consisted mainly of tea. *The Gentleman's Magazine* thought that estimate was conservative and put the total at 4551 horse-loads each consisting of 1½ cwt of tea, or about 21 gallons of brandy or Geneva.

In addition to official figures there is also a detailed account from a very credible eye witness. Vast quantities of contraband were being moved along the old Roman road leading from the Suffolk coast towards Stowmarket. Until major road-building programmes began in the 1790s, the Roman roads that crisscrossed the country were the only reliable way of transporting heavy wagons. The condition of other roads was generally appalling, and worst in winter when carts often foundered in the mud.

The progress of these juggernauts was only sporadically interrupted by the Preventive Authorities but they did not go unnoticed by others. This convenient well-used route passed through Earl Soham, 15 miles from the coast at Sizewell. During the second half of the eighteenth century, the village was home to surgeon William Goodwin who lived at Street Farm.

Goodwin's house had a clear view of the Roman road and of the junction where a lane leads off to Brandeston village. In his journal, which has miraculously survived and is held in the Suffolk Record Office, he meticulously recorded details of contraband convoys passing through Earl Soham from Sizewell Bay to points farther west.

Street Farm, Earl Soham, home to surgeon William Goodwin, during the second half of the eighteenth century.

Entries for February 1785 include: '*2500 Gallons of smuggled Spirits were carried thro' this village in 20 carts within the last six days*' and '*Feb 16 Five Smuggling Carts past through this village at 8 this morning loaded with 150 tubs of Spirits containing 600 Gallons.*'

Using carts or pack ponies porters who delivered contraband to customers were paid a guinea a day.

He notes that though another five carts of spirits passed through a week later he had heard that '*The Soldiers*' had been successful in seizing six such carts and their loads of spirits. They had another success on 2 March: '*15 Carts, 40 horses & 600 Tubs of Spirits were seized this day at Sizewell by a party of Dragoons together with some Tea & bale goods, notwithstanding which ye smugglers worked another cotter at ye same place the ensuing night.*'

Country Estates and Contraband Churches

Although smugglers made life's little luxuries generally available to a larger population their main customers came from the rich elite. However, the people with money were the same people who were responsible for law and order and proper administration of local government.

Many of these leading citizens, including magistrates, lawyers, bankers and landed gentry were prepared to turn a blind eye to the figures who slipped along in the darkness, leaving consignments of tea or gin or what-you-will by the gate or on the step: *Brandy for the Parson, 'Baccy for the Clerk, Laces for a lady...*

Servants in the big houses often played a useful liaison role as they were known to the smugglers or even related to them. Certain clergymen in Suffolk, many whom came from the top families, took turning a blind eye to the extreme. Churches across the county were regularly used as contraband stores.

Customs Riding Officers and Dragoons

Throughout the eighteenth century, when most of the King's Men were engaged in overseas wars, smugglers had it very much their own way. The main threat to the contraband lander and his team came from Customs Riding Officers who had the unenviable job of patrolling the coast on the lookout for signs of smuggling activity; a lonely task made worse by the active resentment of much of the local population. The pay was poor and an officer was expected to be out in all weathers patrolling at least 4 miles of coastline and keeping watch up to 10 miles inland. Many Riding Officers died as a result of violence or under suspicious circumstances.

There are many accounts of clashes between Suffolk smugglers and Customs Officers supported by Dragoons but in the vast majority of incidents the law men were so outnumbered effective prevention was hopeless.

Although some gallant and honest men were among the Customs' Riding Officers, many were open to bribery.

With a great many able-bodied men fighting overseas the Preventive Service was frequently undermanned. Those who did take on the lonely job of Riding Officer were principally recruited from ex-cavalry soldiers. Although there were some gallant and honest men among them, they were always criticised and many were open to bribery. Lax supervision permitted some to retain their jobs (and the pay attached) until they were eighty years of age and quite useless for chasing smugglers.

On 14 January 1764 the *Ipswich Journal* reported: '*On Tuesday, part of General Howard's Dragoons marched into this town; and we hear different Parties of them will be stationed at Stowmarket, Woodbridge, Saxmundham and Walton, in order to check the proceedings of the Smugglers.*'

For much of the second half of the eighteenth century Dragoons were a familiar and colourful sight in a number of villages along the Suffolk coast.

For much of the second half of the eighteenth century Dragoons were a familiar and colourful sight in a number of villages along the Suffolk coast and it was the practice to billet them in pairs in public houses. A

great many of the people whom they lived amongst were directly or indirectly involved in smuggling and resented their presence. Consequently it was generally an undesirable posting.

Stationing the troops as far as possible outside their own counties was an additional precaution so they would not be called on to fight friends or relations.

Impressive black Dragoon musicians took part in recruitment drives at local pubs.

Perhaps a few soldiers found compensation for a generally cold reception in warmer responses from some local country girls. The Dragoon's uniform was impressive and the men must have cut fine figures when compared with the average Suffolk swain.

The black and white illustration included here is interesting for several reasons. It shows a party of Light Dragoons making use of a pub as a recruiting station. A hapless country lad tries on a helmet and sabre to the despair of his sweetheart. Exotically dressed musicians were an aid to recruiting, which explains the black trumpeter in the background observing events.

Tobias Gill, a Negro drummer in Sir Robert Rich's Regiment of 4th Dragoons, was part of a detachment sent to Blythburgh in 1750. On the last Monday of June, Ann Blakemore, a Walberswick girl was found dead on the Walks about a mile west of Blythburgh Village. Gill was accused of murdering her and found guilty by a Coroner's Jury at the Bury St Edmunds Assizes in August and was sentenced to be executed at Blythburgh.

On 14 September 1750, vigorously protesting his innocence, Tobias was led to the gallows. Seeing the London Mail coach approaching he begged the noose be put round his neck and the other end of the rope tied to the coach so he might have a chance to run for his life. His unconventional plea was dismissed and he was executed. His corpse was hung in chains at the four crossways. It was realised too late that Ann Blakemore's body bore no signs of injury and Blythburgh people began to question what really happened. Could it have been the girl wandering along the Walks that June evening had never seen a Negro before? Had she suddenly been confronted with the towering black faced figure and simply died of fright?

The End Game

Prime Minister William Pitt whose tax reform ended tea smuggling overnight.

In 1783, aged only twenty-four, William Pitt the Younger became Prime Minister. After consulting with the great and good of the tea trade, he decided to slash the tax on tea, and compensated for revenue lost, by hugely increasing the window tax. This property-based toll was much easier to enforce and much fairer to the population in general. The bigger house you could afford the more tax paid. Some house owners bricked up windows to reduce the burden; a legacy which can still be seen today in towns and cities.

At a stroke the act reduced the tax on tea from 119 % to 12.5 % and smuggling tea ceased to be profitable; consequently this aspect of the smuggling trade virtually vanished overnight. The consumption of taxed tea rocketed so much that even with the reduced tax rate, the revenue total was soon restored. Thus, coupled with the increase in window tax, the Exchequer revenues actually increased overall.

The legacy of William Pitt's huge increase in window tax can still be seen in today's towns and cities.

This new situation did not put smugglers out of business it just shifted the emphasis on the type of goods they carried. Two years later, in February 1785, William Goodwin noted five carts carrying 600 gallons of spirits passed in the course of just one morning. On 23 February the smugglers were not so lucky, and they lost six carts loaded with spirits to the Preventive Services. During the summer Goodwin saw 20 carts pass by his house in less than a week carrying 2500 gallons of spirits.

After the Battle of Waterloo in 1815 the attention of the armed services was now directed to the home front and combating domestic smuggling. In 1817 the Royal Navy began using blockade techniques preventing smuggling vessels reaching the English coast and in 1831 the Coastguard Service was formed, becoming part of the Royal Navy.

Theberton church near Sizewell where contraband was hidden under the altar cloth.

From 1831 terraces of Coast-guard cottages like these at Sizewell became a familiar sight in Suffolk.

The grip of Coastguards gradually tightened and they were eventually stationed all along the coast. Terraces of Coastguards' cottages overlooking the beaches are now a familiar sight in Suffolk. This initiative, together with a gradual relaxation in taxation on the smugglers' favoured goods, saw the decline and eventual demise of the 'Golden Age' of smuggling.

The Smugglers' Pub

In English maritime counties the nerve centre of smuggling operations was predominantly the local pub. It was here that plots were hatched, arrangements for transportation agreed and runs commissioned. The smugglers' pub served as a meeting place, recruitment centre, secret storage facility, distribution depot and valued customer.

The cosy fifteenth-century *Golden Key* at Snape where many a smuggler's conference would have taken place.

This book explores smuggling connections of Suffolk down the whole of the eastern seaboard from the northern border with Norfolk to the southern border with Essex. It is a guide to a significant number of authentic pubs patronised over two and a half centuries ago by Suffolk smugglers. Many of the landlords of the featured pubs were smugglers themselves.

These wonderful old buildings with their low-beamed ceilings, flagstone floors, inglenook fireplaces and secret hiding places are where, with a little imagination, one can sense the desperate days of the free traders.

Hadleigh
The George
52 High Street, Hadleigh IP7 5AL

Tel: 01473 822151

www.thegeorgehadleigh.co.uk

The George enjoys a commanding position half way along Hadleigh's historic High Street.

There has been a recorded settlement in Hadleigh since the first century and for a time it was renowned as the richest Suffolk woollen cloth town in the region. Its name is said to derive from the Norse word 'Haethlega', meaning the heath covered place. Hadleigh has retained much of its natural beauty whilst evolving into a delightful small market town. Various

The inn sign depicts King George I, who was the first of the Hanoverian Kings.

17

styles of cottages, shops and houses huddle together in a pleasing mix of periods.

In a book of smugglers' exploits in a coastal county like Suffolk it might seem curious to begin with an inland town 40 miles from the sea. However, surprising as it might seem, Hadleigh was Suffolk's major centre for this illegal activity and has given its name to one of the most 'successful' smuggling gangs.

The impressive original beamed ceiling in the front bar dates back to at least 1537.

The banditti from this area were part of the countywide army of land-based smugglers and, just as in the military, logistics was their area of expertise. At its height the Hadleigh Gang could readily muster a minimum of 100 men at short notice, with twice that number of carts, horses and pack ponies at their disposal. Put simply, logistics is the planning of management of the flow of goods, services or information from a

point of origin to waiting customers. In practice it is a complex operation requiring detailed organization.

In the Hadleigh case the point of origin for goods was a number of strategic locations along the Suffolk shore. Extensive open beaches run the length of the county's coast and favoured collection points for contraband shipped from the continent were the beaches at Benacre and Covehithe in the north and Dunwich and Sizewell further south.

The whole enterprise was demand driven and Hadleigh smugglers were mostly engaged in supplying tea, brandy and Geneva gin to people with ready money across the county. The greatest demand came from owners of large country estates and the professional classes in towns like Beccles, Bungay and Ipswich but the gang's customer base spread as far as London itself and on occasion they

Good food at reasonable prices is served in the separate dining room with a selection of popular homemade favourites.

linked up with the notorious Hawkhurst Gang from Kent *(see page 83).*

A picture of the Hadleigh Gang's activities and size of their operations can be gleaned from detailed Custom House records including reports like the following, from the middle of the eighteenth century:

The large patio garden, formerly the inn's stable yard, catches the sun all day.

'20 May: 70 horses with dry goods landed at Sizewell; 27 May: 27 horses with wet goods and; 36 loaded with tea landed at Sizewell; 11 June: 60 horses most with brandy, 53 with tea; 2 July: 83 horses with tea, 9 waggon loads wet goods; 12 July: 50 horses, tea. 17 Sept: 120 horses — 100 smugglers; 10 Nov: 50 horses dry goods, 1 cart w/wet goods; 23 Nov: at least 40 horses, mostly dry goods.'

Traditional cask ales are from the Greene King range with additional genuine specials.

At the height of their dominance the gang's leader was family man John Harvey who had four sons and two daughters. He lived in an Elizabethan house called Pond Hall which still stands amid ponds set back from the road to Duke Street.

During this time countless varieties of contraband were carried through the town on horses and carts and meetings took place secretly behind locked doors. There are rumours of underground passages leading to various locations and rooftop escape routes for free traders. Cellars, attics and even former priests' hidey holes were all used for concealing contraband caches. G. P. R. James in *The Smugglers* describes the situation:

Attached houses in Angel Street provided escape routes for smugglers through linked attics and across the roofs.

'Many streets had private passages from one house to another, so the gentleman inquired for by the officers at No. 1, was often quietly walking out of No. 20, while they were searching for him in vain. The back of one street had always excellent

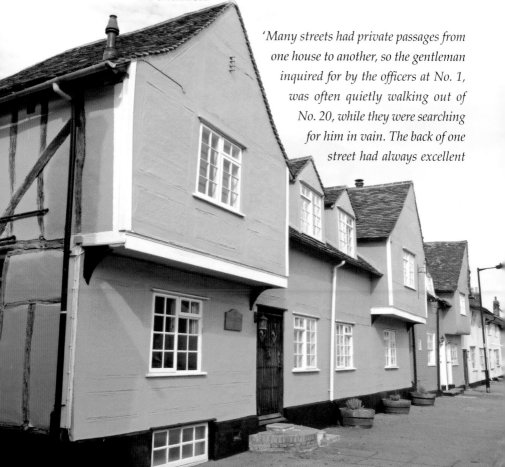

means of communication with the front of another, and in the gardens gave exit to the country with as little delay as possible.'

One of the Hadleigh Gang's biggest battles with the authorities happened in 1735. Customs Officers and military had infiltrated their numbers and discovered the location of one of their contraband stores in a cottage at Semer, 3 miles northwest of the town.

The Preventive Men transported the huge stockpile of tea back to The George Inn for temporary safekeeping. When the gang heard about this outrage they sent in a detachment to demand their 'bounty' back. After a bloody encounter where lives were lost, the felons recovered their loot and rode off into the night. However the authorities recognized a large number of the offenders and reprisals eventually followed.

Harvey, with other members of the gang stood trial for smuggling on 22 June 1747. John Wilson and John Biggs were convicted of firing pistols during the affray of twelve years

John Harvey, one of the leaders of the Hadleigh Gang, lived here at Pond Hall on the outskirts of the town.

earlier. They were hanged on Gallows Hill at the far end of the High Street for their part in the audacious crime. John Harvey's death sentence was commuted to seven years transportation. Bribery may have played a part in the reduction of his sentence and the fact he returned to Hadleigh within the period and reputedly back to his old ways!

The George, a former coaching inn dating back to at least 1537, enjoys a commanding position half way along Hadleigh High Street close to the impressive parish church of St Mary's. Picturesque and welcoming, the old inn functions as a true community hub with a home-from-home feeling often missing in town pubs these days.

The large single bar with its impressive original beamed ceiling looks out directly onto the historic High Street with its colourful mix of architectural styles. Good food at reasonable prices is served in the separate dining room with a selection of popular homemade favourites. Traditional cask ales are from the Greene King range with additional genuine specials. The large patio garden, formerly the inn's stable yard, catches the sun all day.

Gallows Hill where Hadleigh Gang members John Wilson and John Biggs were hanged.

Blythburgh
The White Hart Inn

London Road, Blythburgh, Halesworth IP19 9LQ

Tel: 01502 478217

www.blythburgh-whitehart.co.uk

Blythburgh village stands a few miles inland from Southwold within the Suffolk Coast and Heaths Area of Outstanding Natural Beauty, known as the Suffolk Sandlings. The tidal section of the River Blyth flows just north of the village on its way out to sea at Southwold Harbour. Over the years the seawalls have been breached and the unreclaimed land has created Blythburgh Water, a tidal lagoon visited by flocks of mud-loving wading birds.

Fire, the scourge of windswept timber and thatch towns, visited Blythburgh several times. The conflagration of 1676 was especially damaging. Some inhabitants, unable or unwilling to rebuild their properties moved elsewhere. Few village buildings standing before that calamitous date now survive. By 1754 there were only 21 households and a population of 124.

The White Hart Inn with its red brick 'Dutch' gable end which was high fashion in the seventeenth century.

The fine inglenook fireplace graces one end of the bar.
Below: Although much of The White Hart's timber frame has disappeared the moulded ceiling is a wonderful feature in the bar.

At this time life for Suffolk farm labourers and their families was bleak. Children worked in the fields from age six and wages were very low in comparison with other counties. The payment for one night's work helping to transport contraband was equivalent to that paid for a week's backbreaking agricultural toil.

The A12 which bisects the village today started life in 1785 as a new turnpike with some of the fabric from the dissolved priory used in its foundations. The highway crosses the Blyth River by a strategic bridge while other roads radiate off in all directions. The village is best known for Holy Trinity church, visible for many miles and celebrated as the Cathedral of the Marshes. After 1785 the old main road that meandered past the church became a quiet backwater.

Today The White Hart is a friendly, roomy, open-plan dining pub with ancient beams, woodwork and staircase.

The 300 or so present population inhabits houses clustered close to the main road and church, or in scattered cottages and farmhouses. Today Blythburgh's modest presence belies its former importance. At the time of the Norman Conquest it was part of the royal estate and one of Suffolk's twelve market towns. Whether the ancient town was ever a significant port like nearby Walberswick or Dunwich is doubtful. In any case seagoing vessels of any size were probably unsuited to the narrow twisting channel leading upstream to Blythburgh.

Waterways provided routes for moving smuggled cargoes inland. The River Blyth served this purpose for goods landed at Southwold and Walberswick. Blythburgh could have been designed for smugglers with the inn situated conveniently between waterway and highway. Here goods ferried upstream from the coast were transferred to carts and pack

Here you will find the perfect combination of comfort and traditional style.

ponies for transportation to secret storage locations and the onward journey to eager customers.

Looking out from the beer garden of The White Hart Inn across the broad expanse of water and marsh it is easy to imagine boats being sculled silently across the lagoon on cloudy nights. An all clear signal was flashed from the little window high in the pub's roof to crews in the flotillas secure in the knowledge that the locality was temporarily free from Preventive Men.

The interesting pebble-built house directly opposite the pub, known today as The Old Custom House, is thought to have ecclesiastical origins dating from the sixteenth century. Built directly into the bank with no rear ground access, this security factor may be part of the reason it had previously been used as a gaol. The present owners Jeff and Wendy Sutton offer B&B.

Only five minutes from Southwold you would expect nothing less than the full range of Adnams traditional ales.

The small window in the roof of The White Hart with a view across the marsh provided a convenient spot for a light signalling all clear to the small boats ferrying contra-band.

Suffolk stone is generally not of sufficient quality for building and consequently supporting cornerstones for important buildings had to be imported at great expense. This also explains why many Suffolk Churches have round towers built with pebbles from the beaches, and accounts for the exis-

The beer garden of the pub looks directly on to the tidal lagoon of Blythburgh Water.

tence of towns like Lavenham where almost all the buildings
are timber framed.

During the optimistic early years of the sixteenth century,
The White Hart Inn functioned as a courthouse. A tunnel

The Old Custom
House directly
opposite the pub
served for a time
as a gaol.

connected it with The Old Custom House. The former
entrance of this underpass can be seen in the pub's cellar
sealed with narrow red bricks.

Although much of the inn's timber frame has disappeared, a
handsome staircase remains and a fine moulded ceiling
survives in the bar. In the seventeenth century the southern
end of the building was replaced by a red brick 'Dutch' gable
which was high fashion at the time. The roadside façade was
originally the back of the building and dates from the nine-
teenth-century. Today The White Hart is a friendly, roomy
open-plan dining pub, with the Dutch gable providing
internal space for the large inglenook fireplace.

A very wide choice of home-cooked dishes ranges from light
bites through traditional pub favourites to fine specials made
from local fresh ingredients and a children's menu. The full
Adnams' range of traditional ales is available. A large rear
patio area and spacious beer garden with picnic sets look
directly on to the tidal lagoon of Blythburgh Water and the
wildlife marshes beyond.

Blyford
Queen's Head

Southwold Road, Blyford, Halesworth IP19 9JY

Tel: 01502 478404

www.queensheadblyford.co.uk

Blyford (Blythford) lies 6 miles northeast of the smugglers' landing beaches at Dunwich and was the perfect resting place for tired horses and men engaged in transporting illegal goods inland. When contraband cargos reached Blyford part of the load was quickly stashed in temporary hiding places in and around the inn including a secret recess inside the pub chimney breast.

All Saints church across the road from the pub was also used as a smugglers' store. It was linked to the Queen's Head by a tunnel accessed through a trap door to the left of the pub's inglenook fireplace. Built in 1088 mainly of flint, the church has two

The beautiful thatched roof of the fifteenth-century pub reflects the living reeds growing in the river valley beyond.

Contraband was stored in a recess above the pub's fireplace and a trap door in the floor to the left of the hearth gave access to a tunnel connecting with the church.
Below: Many a smugglers' conference would have taken place in this cottage pub.

Norman doors and a perpendicular English tower. The font was added later in the thirteenth century. Another church, St Andrew's at Westhall, some 3 miles north, provided an even better-kept secret. Here kegs were hidden in the valley roof, between the two ridges.

Simple country-style furniture stands on the wooden floor of the adjacent separate dining room.

In the middle of the eighteenth century the landlord here was John Key, who became leader of the local free traders. This enterprising publican eventually made sufficient money from smuggling to give up the licensed trade altogether. Moving to Beccles he took a house at Swine's Green on Smugglers' Lane near St Anne's Road: *'Where five crossways meet'*.

There are a number of anecdotes associated with John Key. One tells of Revenue Officers catching up with him 6 miles south of his home as he was returning from a smuggling run. They spotted him near St Peter's church Brampton riding a horse he had borrowed for the occasion. John spurred his mount on but, nearing the Duke of Malborough Inn at Weston, one of the officers shot his horse from under him.

Scrambling from the saddle he ran across the fields and completed the journey to arrive just before the King's men. To his delight, he found a very similar horse grazing contentedly near his home. He hurriedly locked the animal into the stable, and donned his nightclothes on top of his working garments. When he heard the inevitable knock on the door, he was able to lean out the window and shout innocently enough *'Wha' d' ye want?'* When the Revenue Men replied *'where's your horse ... didn't we shoot him less than half an hour ago?'* John directed them to the stable, and his equine alibi.

The Queen's Head continues the tradition of keeping pigs and chickens as did all country pubs during the era of the free traders.

In keeping with Suffolk's history, the inn sign features the head of the fifteenth-century Queen known as St Etheldreda.

A number of Suffolk churches were used for contraband concealment but the curate in this illustration seems to be apologizing to the concerned parson for smugglers exceeding agreed limits.

The George at Hadleigh and The White Hart at Blythburgh are both purpose built inns but the Queen's Head at Blyford evolved organically from fifteenth-century farm cottages into the lovely old thatched pub we see today. Particularly special is part of its surrounding landholding still used to raise pigs and chickens and to grow vegetables and salad, just as it would have been six hundred years ago.

The inn sign of the Queen's Head features St Etheldreda, who was born in AD 636 at Exning in Suffolk, 12 miles east-north-east of Cambridge. She was the third and most celebrated of the saintly daughters of King Anna of East Anglia, by his wife, Saewara.

The spacious car park and beer garden were originally part of the pub's productive small holding.

Run by Shaun and Lauren Doig, this is a true country pub beautifully situated in the Blyth Valley, about 3 miles south of the town of Halesworth on the road to Southwold. Built around the fifteenth century the pub retains many original features including the impressive thatched roof reflecting the living reeds growing in the river valley beyond. With a large beer garden and plenty of surrounding green space, the pub is ideal for relaxing outside on a warm summer day, while in the winter, a log fire provides a warm and cosy atmosphere.

The earliest recorded reference to The King's Head is in a lease granted to George Cocke, dated 1668.

Beccles
The King's Head
4-6 New Market, Beccles NR34 9HA

Tel: 01502 718730

Located in the far north of the county the bustling market town of Beccles stands close to the beautiful Broads National Park's southern edge. The River Waveney, formerly a smugglers' highway, still wends its way through the town. Contraband landing places along the river now provide short-stay moorings for today's pleasure boat visitors.

In 1718 the Yarmouth Surveyor of Customs attended Beccles Quarter Session held at The King's Head Inn with the purpose of prosecuting smuggler Coe Arnold of Lowestoft. A conviction by a jury, who were probably all involved in smuggling or benefiting from it, was highly unlikely – and so it proved. The diligent Preventive Officer reported he found:

> 'such a great number of local Justices of the Peace and so great a crowd of people from Lowestoft supporting Arnold, all declaring that officers could not search any man on ye road without ye assistance of a constable… that your Honrs. Officers were advised to withdraw ye suit.'

Coe Arnold had been apprehended following a pursuit through the streets of Beccles. Dashing through the White Lyon Yard with a quantity of contraband: *'He threw his bags over a "rail" or fence and a man called Sallows carried them away without offering or calling for help.'* The judge directed the jury that all was properly proved but the twelve good men of Beccles brought in a not guilty verdict. The Collector commented: *'this showed how little respect they had… for His Majesty, His revenue and His Officers.'*

Present day Wash Lane in Beccles, formerly known as Smugglers' Lane, was an artery along which contraband moved into the town from river landing points at Barnby and Worlingham. Illicit cargoes also arrived along the road from Covehithe and Benacre; favourite landing spots of the Hadleigh Gang.

For centuries stagecoaches entered the galleried cobbled yard through the open archway which is now the main entrance.

In the middle of the eighteenth century, John Key former landlord of the Queen's Head at Blyford (*see previous entry*)

Outside seating is provided in the pedestrianised area along Sheepgate Street.

moved to Beccles. The house, probably spotted by Key when he was helping to move cargoes landed at Dunwich, was adjacent to a large barn. Both buildings had numerous places for hiding contraband. Still standing in 1931, the buildings were described as being in dilapidated condition. Today the

The inn was refurbished and reopened by J. D. Wetherspoon in February 2013.

lane leads to the Ellough Estate, and on past Castle Farm to Codlins or Codling Wood where there was once a dump for contraband between Ellough Road and the Worlingham boundary.

At a Weatherspoon's pub you are always guaranteed to find an excellent selection of real ales.

Things did not end well for Key. On a night in March 1745 members of the Beccles smuggling gang, suspecting him of being an informer, entered his house and pulled him out of bed. They whipped him with considerable ferocity, dragged him into the street, tied him naked to a horse and rode off with him into the night. The Excise Commissioners offered a substantial reward of £50 for the discovery and conviction of anyone concerned but no one came forward and Key was never seen again.

The inn we see today almost certainly replaced an even earlier building as Beccles was ravaged by a great fire which swept through the town on the evening of 29 November 1586 and: '*raged with the greatest violence in the vicinity of New Market*'. As with most medieval English towns, Beccles endured several fires in the 1660s so it seems likely, even if The King's Head

The former White Lyon in Market Street stands next to the Public Halls Theatre.

had survived the earlier conflagration, it would have burned down around this time.

The earliest recorded reference to The King's Head is in a lease granted to George Cocke dated 1668. Today the Grade II listed building is described as: *'seventeenth and eighteenth centuries, with alterations'*. The eighteenth-century, Georgian-style portions flank the earlier sections. In 1671, two decades after the end of the English Civil War, Cocke became the inn's first landlord when he was granted: *'the tenement in the cornerstead of the Market'*.

During the centuries that followed stagecoaches clattered and jingled their way through the open archway which is now the main pedestrian access. Here they entered the cobbled yard

which had galleries at the back and extensive stabling further to the rear.

The inn was refurbished and re-opened by J. D. Wetherspoon in February 2013. Whilst sympathetically retaining the traditional character of the building, its restoration has modernised facilities providing high levels of style and comfort in the bar, dining areas and guest rooms.

Ferocious retribution was meted out by smugglers to suspected informers.

Southwold
Swan Hotel

Market Place, Southwold IP18 6EG

Tel: 01502 722186

www.theswansouthwold.co.uk

Southwold is a charming north Suffolk seaside town on the Heritage Coast at the mouth of the River Blyth famous for its colourful beach huts. It is almost an island, being bounded by the North Sea to the east, the River Blyth and Southwold Harbour to the south-west and by Buss Creek to the north. There is just one road in and out, approached through neighbouring Reydon.

In 1720, just before Christmas, Mr Davis the Customs Collector at Southwold together with his deputy David Lanham plus William Knott and two Boatmen were coming into

Adnams' flagship establishment enjoys a good location on the High Street, close to the seafront, and just yards from the brewery.

Southwold haven when their boat capsized. Only William Knott was rescued: the Southwold Custom House was stripped of its senior staff at a stroke. Presumably Southwold smugglers didn't shed any tears.

In 1729 it was noted that *'French vessels hovering on the coast between this place and Newcastle'* were selling brandy to colliers and other local boats going about their lawful business. In 1778 a detachment of Lord Orford's Norfolk regiment camped at Southwold fought a battle with smugglers when a 12-gun cutter tried to make a landing under cover of bombardment. Reinforcements arrived and all the goods were seized.

The lounge next to the entrance and reception area, is a comfortable mish-mash of sofas and chairs grouped around coffee tables.

On 25 July 1793 The Revenue cutter *Hunter* engaged a smuggling lugger in Southwold Bay. In the fight two of the cutter's

men were so seriously injured they were taken ashore and carried to the Old Swan Inn (now the Swan Hotel). One of them, John Davey, died the following day. His shipmate, Thomas Cousins, died shortly afterwards and they were both buried at the same time.

Another Southwold Customs Officer called Swayne (a contemporary of William Woodward and Benjamin Lowsey who were thrown into the sea by smugglers at Dunwich), observed a smuggling cutter becalmed at daybreak in South-wold Bay. The large lug sails hung flat and, although using her sweeps as oars, the vessel was not able to escape. The Preventive Men under Swayne soon overtook the smugglers in their galley, when the smuggler hailed with *'Keep off, Swayne, without you wish for bloodshed; we are fully armed and mean to fight'*.

The spacious dining room, at the back, is elegant and well-lit contributing to the hotel's reputation as the 'Grande Dame' of Southwold.

The ready wit of the officer saved the situation. The recognition had been mutual, and Swayne, calling the smuggler by name said: '*I will come on board myself and will speak to you alone*'. He did so but in catching hold of the halliards drew his knife across them, and down came the sail. Upon seeing this the smuggler called on his men to surrender.

One can opt for a simple main course with a pint of Adnams or glass of wine in the bar.

Swayne was a zealous officer, whom nature had equipped with unusually large feet, which left tell-tale imprints in the sand, as recognisable as his face to smugglers who operated in the area for which he was responsible. They usually examined the sand at night to see if he was about, and he had been known to walk backwards from Misner Haven to Sizewell Sluice to deceive them, then conceal himself in a depression in the shingle and wait for men on the beach to give the signal for a 'crop' to be landed. At the right moment he would spring up brandishing a horse pistol.

The Swan, Adnams' flagship establishment, was rebuilt in 1659 following the Great Fire. It was remodelled in 1826 and further additions made in 1938. It stands in a prominent position on the High Street, close to the seafront, and just yards from the brewery. Outlooks from the large, family-friendly rooms include a view of the town's picturesque lighthouse.

The hotel, which is highly welcoming in a rather old-fashioned way, is renowned locally for its traditional and French influenced cuisine. The lounge, next to the entrance and reception area, is a comfortable mishmash of sofas and chairs grouped around coffee tables. The spacious dining room, at the back, is elegant and well-lit contributing to the hotel's reputation as the 'Grande Dame' of Southwold.

The à la carte dinner menu may include pork fillet with Parma ham, or steamed seabass followed by lemon cheesecake or mango custard tart. Lunch is served in the restaurant, or one can opt for a simple main course with a pint of Adnams or glass of wine in the bar.

On 25 July 1793 The Revenue cutter *Hunter* engaged a smuggling lugger in Southwold Bay.

During the eighteenth century pitched battles were fought here between smugglers and Revenue Men.

Southwold
The Harbour Inn

Black Shore, Southwold IP18 6TA

Tel: 01502 722381

www.harbourinnsouthwold.co.uk

Southwold was a prosperous fishing port from the eleventh century up until the First World War. The harbour a bustling place with a fascinating collection of maritime workshops and fishing enterprises, lies half-a-mile southwest of the main town centre, beyond Gun Hill and South Green.

The sale of freshly caught fish still attracts many visitors to the harbour which can be reached, either along Blackshore

Road or Ferry Road or by the reliable ferry from Walberswick. There is also pedestrian access to Walberswick beyond The Harbour

Overlooking (and sometimes in!) the River Blyth, flooding can be a problem during winter months so it's as well to come prepared with wellies!

Inn and the Bailey bridge with excellent view of the harbour area.

Convicted smuggler George Butcher, who for a time owned The Harbour Inn, operated during the latter part of the smuggling era. Trading as a coal and seed merchant, he lived in Hill House, at the top of Blyford Lane, in Wenhaston village, 5 miles inland from Southwold. Contraband he brought in through the harbour was taken up the River Blyth and landed at Wenhaston Bridge. From here Butcher sent it on by carrier to Ipswich or to his brother-in-law, a draper in Norwich.

In 1855 an unsigned letter was delivered to Thomas Greenwood, vicar of Wenhaston expressing concern about a certain

The Harbour Inn as the smugglers would have known it.

The harbour is a bustling place with a fascinating mix of maritime workshops and fishing enterprises.

inhabitant of the village, who the writer claimed, had been smuggling for twenty-five years. In his letter the writer advised the vicar that the man in question, whom he refused to name in fear of himself being killed, possessed a wherry, horses, carts, his own men and was at one time landlord of The Harbour Inn at Southwold.

There are also several references to Butcher and his commercial activities recorded in the diaries of James Maggs, a Southwold schoolmaster, auctioneer and general factotum. The most damaging entry was recorded on 30 November 1855, when Maggs escorted George Butcher to Ipswich Gaol for smuggling.

The tower of Southwold church stands tall beyond the marsh.

At the time of his conviction Butcher was fifty-two, and described as 5 feet 4 inches in height with a fresh complexion,

It is possible to follow the historical journey of this infamous hostelry through the pictures, photographs and memorabilia decorating the walls of the bar.
Below: Cheerful staff serve a choice of 16 wines by the glass, along with Adnams Southwold, Broadside and Ghost Ship on handpump.

brown hair and hazel eyes. He was married with two children, at the time of his arrest, who were aged twenty-five and twenty-one. Charged with offences against Customs he was taken to Ipswich Gaol on 1 December 1855 to serve a sentence of nine months.

At the same time a man called Forman from Wenhaston, undoubtedly a member of Butcher's gang, was charged with the same offence and given a similar sentence. On his release George Butcher returned home and carried on with his legitimate business until his death aged seventy-one in 1875.

Picnic-sets on the terrace in front of the pub overlook boats on the Blyth estuary.

In the early 1700s The Harbour Inn was known as 'Blackshore Alehouse'. By the end of the century it was being referred to as 'The Fishing Buss' or simply 'The Buss'. Its ownership and management in the eighteenth and early-nineteenth centuries were closely linked with the ownership and management of the Blackshore Quay and wharf which it served.

During winter months flooding can be a threat in this traditional old smuggler's pub overlooking the River Blyth, so it's as well to come prepared with wellies!

The Harbour Inn has a friendly and relaxed atmosphere welcoming families and well-behaved dogs. Two wood panelled, snug and cosy bars are on different levels. In the nautical themed top bar, with its wood burning stove, it is possible to follow the historical journey of this infamous hostelry through the pictures, photographs and memorabilia displayed on its walls.

The large, elevated dining room has panoramic views of the harbour, lighthouse, brewery and churches beyond the marshes. The lower front bar, with tiled floor and panelling,

Tables behind the pub overlook the marshy commons towards the town half-a-mile away.

is broadly similar to the top bar except that staff here must stoop to serve pints of Adnams through a hatch. Picnic-sets on the terrace in front of the pub overlook boats on the Blyth estuary while seats and tables behind the pub overlook the marshy commons to the town half-a-mile away.

Fish dishes take high priority and the menu begins with little taster dishes to 'pick, mix and share' – potted shrimps, cockle popcorn and roll herrings being just three. Other fishy offerings include grilled spiced mackerel fillet, or clam, king prawn, smoked haddock and potato chowder. Meat eaters are catered for with dishes such as pulled beef brisket in a toasted brioche bun with BBQ sauce. Cheerful staff serve a choice of 16 wines by the glass, along with Adnams Southwold, Broadside and Ghost Ship on handpump.

The sale of freshly caught fish still attracts many visitors to the bustling harbour.

The 600-year-old Bell Inn is situated in the heart of the picturesque seaside village of Walberswick, a stone's throw from the rolling dunes and harbour.

Walberswick
The Bell Inn
Ferry Road, Walberswick IP18 6TN

Tel: 01502 723109

www.bellinnwalberswick.co.uk

This idyllic coastal settlement meanders downhill to the village green and southern foreshore at the mouth of the River Blyth and is a particularly popular destination for those who enjoy walking, cycling and bird watching. The much higher profile town of Southwold stands a mile away on the north side of the estuary.

Coastal erosion and the shifting of the river mouth meant the neighbouring town of Dunwich, 3 miles south, was lost as a port in the last years of the thirteenth century. Following a brief period of rivalry and dispute with Dunwich,

Walberswick became a major trading port from that time until the First World War. Today only small fishing boats and pleasure craft frequent the river and almost half of the properties in the village are holiday homes.

During the early eighteenth century Customs' reports and requests for additional support were sent almost daily to the London Headquarters. The following report of 1715 highlights the extent of smuggling in and around Walberswick and indicates where pubs like The Bell and The Anchor obtained their supplies:

The Bell is full of character with quirky snugs, beamed ceilings, hidden alcoves and this wonderful old curved settle.

Furnishings include cushioned pews, window seats, and scrubbed pine tables.

'*Whereas it has been a frequent practice for french sloops to come upon the coast of Suffolk and particularly to Dunwich where they land quantities of wine and brandy so that gentlemen and Publick Houses are filled therewith (as we are told) and the officer at Southwold cannot come thither without riding seven miles about so that the Crown hath suffered much thereby*

The charming rambling bar of the sixteenth-century Bell Inn presents a chronicle of pub flooring through the centuries.

– we humbly propose as a remedy thereof that a boat with two able boatmen and under the direction of a proper officer were fixed at Walberswick which would serve not only Southwold Haven but also Dunwich and the places adjacent.'

The present Anchor Inn, on the approach to Walberswick, stands a little further back from the site of the earlier pub of

The Bell offers a wealth of Suffolk character with quirky snug corners.

Today only small fishing boats and pleasure craft frequent the river and almost half of the properties in the village are holiday homes.

that name which was long known as a smuggling haunt. In the 1920s, during demolition of the original inn, workmen found a bricked-up doorway in the remains of the cellar. When the new pub's water supply was laid on traces of an underground passage were discovered leading from the cellars of the original inn towards the beach. 'Bell Cottage' was said to be connected by a tunnel to the old vicarage near the ferry, part of which was discovered when building work was carried out.

The present day Anchor Inn stands near the site of the original old smugglers' pub.

The 600-year-old Bell Inn is situated in the heart of Walberswick, near the village green and a stone's throw from the sea. It is a perfect all-year-round destination. During colder months there are roaring open fires and hearty home cooked meals. In summer visitors enjoy al fresco dining in the popular, family friendly garden which overlooks the beach.

The interior of this lovely old pub has a number of characterful seating areas with historic features including oak-beamed ceilings and hidden alcoves. The charming rambling bar presents a chronicle of pub flooring through the centuries, with

The Bell is situated in an area of outstanding natural beauty blest with big blue skies and refreshing sea air.

Walberswick as the
smugglers would
have known it.

sagging ancient bricks, broad boards, flagstones and an area with black and red tiles. Furnishings are similarly diverse, including antique curved settles, cushioned pews and window seats, scrubbed tables and two huge fireplaces, one with a welcoming, elderly, winter wood-burning stove.

The cuisine includes a varied choice of delicious freshly prepared, home-cooked meals with locally sourced ingredients. Firm favourites on the menu are deep-fried breaded whitebait, Suffolk smokies, steak, ale and mushroom short-crust pastry pie, plus apple and cinnamon pannacotta crumble all accompanied with perfectly kept Adnams beers and wines.

Huge quantities of contraband passed this way on misty moonlit nights.

Dunwich
The Ship

St James's Street, Dunwich, Saxmundham IP17 3DT

Tel: 01728 648219

www.shipatdunwich.co.uk

Formerly called the Barne Arms, the pub was part of the estate owned in the smuggling days by Michael Barne.

A tiny single-street hamlet surrounded by acres of nature reserves and heathland, a cluster of houses incorporating a perfect pub and an excellent small heritage museum, an unspoilt shingle beach stretching to infinity, the atmospheric ruins of a clifftop monastery that inspired Turner and there you have what remains of Dunwich today. Over the past eight centuries the greater part of this former prosperous maritime town has been swallowed by the sea.

A brick-arched fireplace on one wall of the traditionally furnished main bar houses a substantial wood burner whose doors are left open on the coldest days.
Below: The simple conservatory which extends the dining capacity overlooks the back terrace and garden.

Once the medieval capital of East Anglia, Dunwich provided housing enough for a population of 3000, around a dozen churches, a market square and a guildhall. Developed initially as a sheltered harbour at the estuary, environmental events including the great storms in 1286 and 1347 caused the Dunwich river to shift its exit north to the River Blyth at Walberswick. Sea defences were not maintained, and Dunwich was largely abandoned as coastal erosion progressively overtook the town.

Melancholy remnants of Greyfriars Monastery hint at the former importance of this once thriving medieval seaport. Permeated by a palpable sense of loss, the ruins carry the realization that within another century, Dunwich may well disappear for good.

The enormous garden with its well-spaced picnic sets is dotted with fruit trees including a 300-year-old fig.

One of the terraced houses extending along from the pub is home to Dunwich Museum which contains an impressive model of the former old town. Another display features local smuggler Elijah Larter, the *'crafty old Dunwich bird'*, who narrates the story of his involvement in the free trade as visitors venture to glimpse him sitting inside his fishing hut.

Throughout the smuggling era Dunwich was a popular contraband landing spot keeping the Revenue cutters busy. In 1778 and 1779 Riding Officers had numerous clashes with the free traders, including one inland chase of 40 miles. In the late 1790s Henry Walters led the Preventive Men in a desperate encounter with Will Laud and his gang at Misner Haven. Laud is the outlaw featured in Reverend Richard Cobbold's 'true' story, *The History of Margaret Catchpole, a Suffolk Girl*.

Walters' men were greatly outnumbered and had to fight a retreat along Dunwich Cliff.

Walters saved himself and his wounded brother Samuel by shooting the white horse from under a determined attacker. One of his men was not quite so fortunate; finding he could not get clear before daylight he hid in a pigsty, and when the smugglers discovered him he was further humiliated by being made to repeat the Lord's Prayer backwards!

In March 1803, at two in the morning, villagers were woken by flashing lights and the sound of gunfire. Britain was at war with France at the time, and people feared the French were about to land. Before the firing ceased a cannon ball hit the stable wall of The Ship Inn. A large vessel was seen sailing

The contraband landing beach, overlooked by the terrace of Coastguard cottages and watch house, is just 100 paces from the front door of The Ship Inn.

Dunwich Museum is housed in a cottage five doors along from the pub.

The main feature in the museum is this model of Dunwich in the twelfth century. The dotted yellow line denotes the present coastline, all buildings below having been lost to the sea.

Elijah Larter seated in his fishing hut narrates Dunwich's smuggling story.

away, while a smaller one, like a fishing smack, crept close to the beach.

The cannon ball bore the British Navy's broad arrow mark but the Admiralty denied any involve-ment or knowledge of the incident. Some villagers naturally thought it had something to do with smuggling but if a run had been planned someone in the village would have known. The puzzling episode remains a mystery to this day.

The Ship Inn is a delightful old pub with a warmly welcoming licensee and friendly staff. It was formerly called the 'Barne Arms', after the family who owned the Dunwich Estate during the smuggling era. The first of the original small cottage rooms, entered by a step down from the hallway, has been opened up to create a large square bar / dining room where a mix of old country furniture stands on the part quarry tiled and part carpeted floor.

There is low settle-style seating around the half panelled light cream walls which are decorated with maritime drawings, paintings and photographs including a framed cigarette card collection displaying the story of navigation. A brick-arched fireplace on one wall houses a substantial wood burner whose doors are left open on the coldest days. Adjoining the bar a fairy-lit conservatory dining room overlooks a covered outside patio area and the enormous garden, dotted with fruit trees including a 300-year-old fig.

The ruins of Greyfriars Monastery are all that remain of this former important maritime town.

The Ship Inn is very dog friendly and has a beguiling atmosphere, no background music just the gentle hum of conversation. It is a freehouse with five real ales on hand pump when I called. The hearty food on offer combines traditional dishes like their legendary hake and chips plus Blythburgh pork belly and ham hock terrine or lamb cutlets served with an individual shepherd's pie.

THE SAGA OF CROCKY FELLOWS
AND CLUMPY BOWLES

Events following the running of a single cargo of Geneva gin through Sizewell Gap ended in both violence and tragedy and linked the following four smugglers' pubs: The Vulcan Arms at Sizewell, The White Horse Inn at Leiston, The Eels Foot Inn at Eastbridge and The Parrot & Punchbowl at Aldringham.

In June 1778 six cart loads of Geneva – about 300 tubs – were run through Sizewell Gap near The Vulcan Arms. They were transported about 2 miles to Leiston Common, entrusted to the care of Crocky Fellows and stored in a barn. Crocky's employer was relaxed about such matters as long as he was assured of brandy, raisins and tea *'without looking for them'*.

A club-footed breeches maker named Clumpy Bowles from Leiston learned about the cache and passed the information to the local Preventive Officer called Reid. Reid immediately sent for two Dragoons billeted at Leiston's White Horse Inn but both soldiers were drunk and in no fit state to assist.

All that remains today of the infamous Sizewell Gap landing site.

The zealous Customs Man then sent a message to The Eels Foot Inn at Eastbridge where another pair of Dragoons were billeted. The landlady here contrived to delay the departure of the soldiers by giving each of them two large glasses of Hollands gin. Imbibing another glass or two for the road they

were soon in no better condition to help than their comrades-in-arms at The White Horse.

The Vulcan Arms Sizewell as the smugglers would have known it.

After further delay, a Preventive force was eventually mustered but on arrival at the barn they found the door securely padlocked. Crocky Fellows, together with Sam Newson of Middleton and a miller called Quids Thornton, managed a fairly effective temporary delaying action.

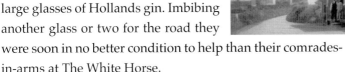

In a gable end of the barn was a wicket door into an adjoining stable loft, with another next to the road at the opposite end. Whilst Fellows, Newson and Thornton had been occupying the attention of the King's Men, a party of about 20 smugglers had been quietly removing the tubs through the two wicket doors and loading them into six two-horse carts. With the work completed Crocky received a covert signal and finally

The smugglers' trail across Leiston Common still shows evidence of cart tracks.

let Preventive Officer Reid and the Dragoons into the barn, whilst the contraband carts trundled away from the far end of the farmyard towards Coldfair Green.

The White Horse Inn at Leiston where two Dragoons were quartered.

The carts remained at Coldfair until midnight when the tubs were transferred to a large vault whose trap door

Billeted Dragoons bored with standby duty were often found to be drunk.

entrance was covered by a muck heap. Bales of tobacco and tea were already stored at one end of the 16' deep vault. By now the exhausted smugglers had been moving the 300 tubs of Geneva from place to place for twenty-four hours. The trap door was dropped into position, muck re-piled on top and all traces of wheel tracks, horses' hooves and human feet were obliterated by driving a flock of sheep in and about the place.

Two more Dragoons were billeted in the quaintly named Eels Foot Inn at Eastbridge.

The next objective was to discover the informer. A fortnight later, around nine o'clock in the evening, two tall men dismounted their horses outside Clumpy's cottage, which stood by a sand pit a short distance from Leiston High Street on the Yoxford Road. Bowles was dragged from his house and flung across the pommel of a saddle. His captors made off at full gallop until they came to a quiet lane near the Green Man at Tunstall.

Bowles gagged with a beer barrel bung fastened in place with his own neckerchief was savagely flogged with riding whips. Finally supposing their victim dead his torturers flung him over a hedge. A farm labourer found him the next morning and he was carried to the pub where events took another dramatic turn.

A servant girl at the Green Man recognised the beer bung used because she had cut a notch in it to remind her which cask it came from. She also remembered lending it to a man named Tom Tibberton. Clumpy recovered sufficiently to confirm Tibberton had been one of his assailants and named the other one as Nosey Debney. Both men were apprehended the following day and subsequently sentenced to two years each in Ipswich Gaol.

The story does not end there because the smugglers eventually wished to recover and distribute the contraband still stored in the vault. They cut through the muck heap and the two youngest, William Cooper and

Retribution against informers usually involved horse whipping.

Robert Debney (Nosey's brother), entered the cellar before letting the foul air escape. When they did not return another smuggler, Black George Nichols, went in after them. Overcome with fumes, he had to be dragged back to the surface.

The original Green Man as the smugglers would have known it.

The present day sign at the new Green Man at Tunstall.

Moving more of the muck and tearing away some of the vault roof the gang began to panic when they realised Cooper and Debney were dead and the Geneva, plus some tea and tobacco, needed to be moved in great haste.

The Parrot & Punchbowl at Aldringham where the contraband was finally seized.

News of the deaths quickly reached a particularly zealous Excise Officer named Engall at Saxmundham. He was the scourge of the local smugglers and knowing the location of a number of the gang's haunts, guessed correctly they would likely be found at the Parrot & Punchbowl. When Engall, flanked by two Dragoons, rode into the yard of the pub he discovered six carts, twelve horses, 300 tubs of Geneva and a gang of smugglers who were finally so demoralised and fatigued they had no will to resist arrest.

The present day Parrot & Punch-bowl retains a great deal of the original character.

The Vulcan Arms is located at Sizewell Gap, close
to Suffolk's most notorious smuggling site.

Sizewell
The Vulcan Arms

Sizewell Gap, Sizewell IP16 4UD

Tel: 01728 830748

www.vulcanarms.freehostia.com

Today there is no trace of the sixteenth-century port of
Sizewell where ships set sail for Iceland Fisheries. According
to John Kirby, *'The Suffolk Traveller'* writing in 1734, Sizewell
had: *'a chapel for divine service and a considerable number of
houses but, at present one farm-house'*. Now it's a quiet atmospheric hamlet standing in the shadow of a nuclear power
station!

Two centuries ago, the landscape around Sizewell appeared
quite different. The sea was flanked by spectacular cliffs, and

the most convenient route through them was via 'Sizewell Gap' which provided ideal natural facilities for free traders in their unlawful pursuits. In the dead of night goods ferried from boats anchored offshore were carried inland along an ancient track-way crossing Westleton Heath. Before completing its onward journey contraband was often hidden in Minsmere levels or stashed in dens and tunnels

Upright timbers separate cosy dining alcoves in the body of the pub.

dug under the soft sandy soils of the Common that lay between Sizewell and Leiston. These excavations were covered with stout planks and concealed by replacing the turf together with pieces of gorse.

The earliest recorded mention of a pub here was in a local census in 1540 which listed Sizewell as being made up of two fishermen, a yeoman farmer and an alehouse. The present

During the smuggling era a tunnel ran from the cellar, below the pool table, through the cliffs to the beach.

Affable landlord Trevor Fisk has owned this free house since 1997.
Below: The Vulcan Arms is a people-friendly, dog-friendly home from home.

The pub shares the beach area with the brooding presence of Sizewell B nuclear power station.

Vulcan Arms is at least 200 years old and almost certainly on the site of its sixteenth-century predecessor.

With the end of the English Civil War Cromwell closed down many of the country's alehouses, the one at Sizewell being among them. From then it became a blacksmith's shop and remained so until the early 1700s when it reverted to being an alehouse/pub. The name given to this second incarnation was The Vulcan Arms, after Vulcan, the Roman God of black-smiths.

Adnams brewery acquired the pub at the beginning of the twentieth century and a plaque on the bar wall lists all land-lords from 1906 to the present day. During the 1980s contrac-tors building Sizewell B power station patronised the pub and it gained a bad reputation with stories of drunkenness and wild behaviour.

In consequence Adnams put it up for sale in 1997, when the present affable landlord Trevor Fisk took it over as a Free House. It has since developed into a quirky, welcoming, dog-friendly place with an extensive menu and a justified reputation for good value food. The one remaining fisherman operating from Sizewell beach supplies Trevor with fresh crabs caught daily.

The pub's award winning sign was designed by landlord Trevor Fisk.

The open-plan modernised interior, leads from a games room with pool table, past the bar and into the body of the pub where upright timbers separate cosy dining alcoves. During the smuggling era a tunnel ran from the cellar, below the pool table, through the cliffs to the beach.

Trevor designed the pub sign himself which won the '*Sign of the Year Award*' in 2010. It depicts three different Vulcans: Mr. Spock from Star Trek who came from the planet Vulcan, Vulcan the Roman god of fire and blacksmith of the gods,

The last of the Sizewell fishermen supplies The Vulcan with fresh crabs.

The Coastguard Watch House still retains a musket rack and formerly held a mortar used to fire a life line to ships in distress off the coast.

plus the Avro-Vulcan delta wing high-altitude strategic bomber. Prior to entering the licensed trade thirty years ago Trevor was a professional musician who still keeps his hand in on Friday nights performing at the pub with his band, *The Symbolics*.

Former Coastguard cottages at Sizewell stand slightly back from the beach.

Leiston
The White Horse
Station Road, Leiston IP16 4HD

Tel: 01728 830694

During the eighteenth century Dragoons were billeted at The White Horse to assist Customs Officers combat smugglers.

Today the rural town of Leiston cum Sizewell has around 5500 residents many of whom probably don't know their neighbours. Back in 1800 the population was around 750 which in effect meant most people knew what was going on. The families involved in smuggling would have been well known and most people, particularly the publicans, would have known when a smuggling run was planned or in progress.

Today pubs change hands with bewildering regularity but in the Georgian period the licensee of a well-known inn was a

noted member of the community, akin to the blacksmith, doctor or parson. Members of the Gildersleeves family, originally from Holland, ran The White Horse Inn at Leiston for over a century from 1732 to 1834.

1772-1776	G. GILDERSLEEVES
1797-1811	A. GILDERSLEEVES
1812-1826	"H. GILDERSLEEVES
1826-1834	G. GILDERSLEEVES
1840-1852	G. W. GOOCH
1853-1854	J. E. ALLEN
1855-1857	E. PEARSON
1858-1863	G. PYM
1864-1885	C. R. UPSON
1886-1898	J. JOHNSON
1899-1903	G. B. SMITH
1904-1922	J. W. POWELL
1923-1929	J. PHILIPS
1930-1933	R. HOOD
1934-1935	A. R. WOODS
1936-1937	F. H. GEORGE
1938-1940	A. GEORGESON
1941-1944	UNLICENSED LAND ARMY HOSTEL
1945-1949	'Chesty' BARBER
1950-1951	S. PRIOR
1952-1953	J. J. McKETT
1954-1955	A. BOWEN
1956	J. WILLIAMS
1957	J. McBRIDE
1958-1963	G. YOUNG
1964-1965	R. LAWLEDGE
1966-1976	L. J. SPIERS
1977-1983	P. JEFFRIES
1984	JOHN & JEAN DOYLE

This plaque in the entrance hall shows members of the Gildersleeves family were licensees at The White Horse for over a century.

In the entrance hall of The White Horse is a chronological list of all the licensees spanning more than 250 years. The second name is Mrs Ann Gildersleeves who may have run the inn for thirty-five years following the death of her husband in 1776 but only officially granted the licence in 1797. Reports suggest she was a popular landlady and valuable ally to Sizewell Gap smugglers.

Ann is reputed to have been a woman of fine physique, great courage and masculine bearing. Because of her ample proportions and voluminous garments she was especially in demand for conveying comparatively small but quite valuable parcels of contraband to various destinations.

Ann stored smuggled goods under the platform of the Quaker Meeting House in Waterloo Road, unbeknown to the worthy Quakers who met there. The original Meeting House, built in 1713, stood on the same site but was replaced in 1860 being then too small.

Situated just a mile inland from Sizewell Gap, Leiston was a focal point for smuggling in eighteenth-century Suffolk. A typical consignment of contraband, passing through Leiston in 1788 consisting mainly of tea was landed here on 15 June,

The basic 'smug-glers' bar at The White Horse.

out of *Cobby's Cutter* at Old Chapel about 2 miles from Sizewell. The cache was packed onto 80 horses while, at the same time, 34 horses were loaded with tea landed out of the *May Flower Cutter* and a further 20 horses were required the following morning to move the remainder of the load.

This contemporary cartoon by Rowlandson shows how female smugglers like Ann Gildersleeves were 'rigged out' to carry contra-band.

There is a suggestion the Hadleigh Gang sometimes worked with the Hawkhurst Gang from Kent and Cobby, who owned the cutter, had been one of the smugglers who broke into the Poole Customs House in Dorset thirty years earlier. He was ultimately hanged and his body displayed on a gibbet at Selsey Bill.

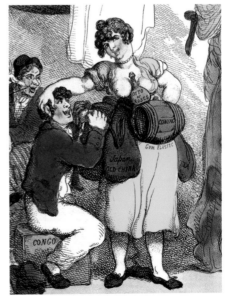

Dragoons were stationed at The White Horse to give support to Customs Men when required. During that 1788 summer two of the soldiers billeted here were called on to assist Customs

Ann stored smuggled goods under the platform of the Quaker Meeting House, unbeknown to the worthy Quakers who met there.

Officer Reid when he heard smugglers had landed 300 tubs of gin and were shipping it inland in six carts but the Dragoons were found to be too drunk to help. This could well have been the result of Ann Gildersleeves generously plying them with liquor to ensure they would not be fit for duty.

At this time it was the practice to hold Coroner's Courts at principal inns and The White Horse may have been the venue for the following report which appeared in *The Ipswich Journal* on 27 June:

> *'There was an inquest at Leiston on Robert Debney and William Cooper who entered a cave used as a repository for smuggled goods, they were suffocated by the stench arising from it, a young man who went to their assistance was very near sharing the same fate, the cave was let down and covered over with horse manure in order to exclude excise officers.'*

This historic eighteenth-century inn offers a basic 'smugglers' bar, restaurant and conservatory plus a good sized beer garden.

The middle of the three cottages became the village pub in the late seventeenth century.

Eastbridge
The Eel's Foot Inn
Leiston Road, Eastbridge IP16 4SN

Tel: 01728 830154

www.theeelsfootinn.co.uk

The pretty hamlet of Eastbridge lies in the heart of the Heritage Coast on the doorstep of the RSPB Minsmere Reserve. The freshwater marshes attract an abundance of birds and butterflies, and a bridleway, once a smugglers' trail, leads through quiet countryside to the sea and links with the Suffolk Coastal Path.

The history and name of The Eel's Foot Inn dates from 1533 when it appears in the parish records as 'an Ale House situated somewhere near the present location'. During the eigh-

A party of the Welch Fusiliers commanded by Lieutenant Dunn warmed themselves by the fire in the winter of 1747. *Below:* The pub doesn't take table bookings but good food is guaranteed.

teenth century it became a smugglers' den and was often the focus of tension between the free traders and the Preventives. At St Peters church, Theberton, a mile or so west of Eastbridge, smugglers concealed contraband kegs beneath the altar cloth.

Already mentioned *(on page 71)* is the 1778 incident, where Dragoons billeted at the inn were plied with spirits by the landlady until they were too drunk to respond to Customs Officer Reid's request for assistance. But another more serious event had occurred thirty years earlier.

On Saturday, 11 December, 1747 a detachment of the Welch Fusiliers commanded by Lieutenant Dunn was ordered to assist Customs Officers in preventing a smugglers' cutter from running goods near Sizewell. The opposing forces

The full range of Adnams ales is available on draught.

In December 1747 this peaceful garden was the scene of a ferocious battle between a detachment of Fusiliers and a gang of 30 well-armed smugglers.

87

clashed here at Eastbridge, when the smugglers offered such spirited resistance the soldiers were forced to retreat to the shelter of The Eel's Foot Inn.

Within half an hour a gang of 30 well-armed banditti rode into the inn yard. Some of them beginning to stable their horses indicated they were no strangers to the place or its proprietor. The Lieutenant ordered his men to drain their tankards and join him outside to confront the smugglers. The free traders responded to his demand for them to surrender by opening fire. When Dunn ordered the Fusiliers to return fire most of the smugglers fled.

Most Suffolk churches were once thatched and the smugglers' storage church of St Peter's Theburton is a rare survivor.

Two of the law breakers were eventually captured and sent to London by sea. For some time it had been the practice to place strong military guards over smugglers who were being moved for fear of escape attempts initiated by their companions. This luckless pair were escorted by two sergeants and twelve private soldiers and sentenced to death at The Old Bailey.

At one time smugglers hid contraband kegs under the altar-cloth in St Peters church, Theberton.

Consisting originally of two cottages, the present Eel's Foot Inn dates from 1642. The third cottage, now the darts room, was added around 1725. Records seem to show the middle one, formerly the cobbler's cottage, became the village pub in the late seventeenth century. The origin of the pub's name is unclear. It may come from 'Heel's Foot', a cobblers' implement, or more likely named after the 'Eel's Boot', a type of woven reed basket used in Eel Fishing.

Because of the unpredictable flow of passing trade from walkers and birders the pub doesn't take meal bookings although they do guarantee to feed visitors even if they might have to wait a short time for a table. Full meals and lighter options are available including fresh fish from Lowestoft plus fresh fruit, vegetables and meat from Suffolk farms complemented by Saxmundham bread.

The rear area where the smugglers' battle took place 270 years ago is now laid out with extensive gardens, patio areas and permanent 'fine weather' barbeque. For younger family members two great pieces of play equipment a 'Ghost Ship' and a 'Traction Engine' provide plenty of entertainment while parents can enjoy a quiet drink.

Aldringham
The Parrot & Punchbowl

Aldringham Lane, Aldringham, Suffolk IP16 4PY
Tel: 01728 830221

The village of Aldringham is located a mile south of Leiston and 3 miles northwest of Aldeburgh. During the eighteenth century Aldringham was a known centre for smuggling and many stories are told of the adventures of local free traders including rough collisions with Excise Officers and Dragoons.

The story that began in June 1778 with 300 tubs of Geneva being run through Sizewell Gap developed to involve several Suffolk pubs and the death of two smugglers by asphyxiation in a contraband storage vault. The sorry tale ended here in Aldringham at The Parrot & Punchbowl.

This pretty country free house built around 1576 was most likely thatched.

Excise Officer Ingall from Saxmundham, on the trail of the gang moving and hiding the contraband knew the location of a number of their haunts and guessed correctly he would likely find them at The Parrot & Punchbowl. On riding into the pub's yard, flanked by two Dragoons, he discovered the booty and the gang so tired they were easily arrested.

There is a rumour persisting to this day of a tunnel leading from The Parrot & Punchbowl to St Andrew's church. This seems highly unlikely as the church is over half-a-mile away across heathlands and through pine woods. It is also a fact that large gangs of smugglers would not have needed a tunnel as they mostly moved openly across the country. However, the free traders did need contraband storage places for which the remote church would have been ideal.

There are loads of beams throughout the up-along-down-along bars and dining areas.

This lovely old feature fireplace enhances the main dining room.

There is light décor throughout and the old country furniture is comfortably cushioned.

The story of a tunnel could have referred to an access shaft excavated in the churchyard leading to a vault under the nave, as was the case in other places. At first sight, the present church is entirely Victorian but a blocked door and lancet in the south chancel wall suggest a probable original date of about 1200, and a rood loft stair buttress also attests to its antiquity. Hanging in the nave is an 1847 painting of the church showing a tall fifteenth-century ruined tower which has now disappeared.

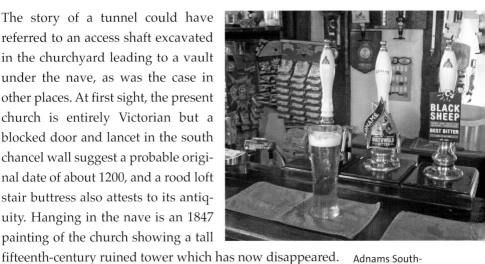

Adnams Southwold is complemented by at least one guest ale.

Inside St Andrew's, by the blocked off chancel priest door, is a mysterious area of concrete in the otherwise wooden floor. The church was consolidated and completely refurbished inside and out in the mid-nineteenth century. Could this be a repair to the collapsed ceiling of a subterranean vault as has been discovered in other churches?

Even in Victorian times the Aldringham roads were unmade and the pub stood in isolation exactly as the smugglers would have known it.

The thatched roof of the old inn has gone and the sixteenth-century pub sign depicting a parrot sitting on a punchbowl has been replaced by something more modern, but much remains of the old 'Aldringham Parrot' to remind visitors of its antiquity.

The pub was built around 1576 when it was curiously called 'The Case is Altered'. The Kemp family, who occu-

This 1847 painting of Aldringham church shows the tall fifteenth-century ruined tower which has now disappeared.

pied the premises throughout the smuggling era from 1604 without a break until 1831, must have been friends of the free traders. It was they who renamed the pub The Parrot & Punchbowl – but no one seems to know why?

This attractive and welcoming old hostelry has loads of beams throughout the up-along-down-along bars and dining areas. When I called it was packed with locals tucking in to helpings of good fairly priced food. Adnams Southwold bitter and Black Sheep from Masham's Yorkshire brewery were on tap.

It is difficult to believe on that day in June 1778, the present lovely sheltered garden was full of Dragoons, Customs Men and smugglers with their attendant horses and cart loads of contraband gin.

Persistent rumours link Aldringham church with a smugglers' tunnel.

This former old farm house has a new look and feel in keeping with modern pubs.

Brandeston
The Queen
The Street, Brandeston IP13 7AD

Tel: 01728 685307

www.thequeenatbrandeston.co.uk

The quiet back lanes winding 6 miles southeast from Earl Soham to Wickham Market pass through Brandeston, Kettleborough and Easton. Any contraband conveyed along this route passed within a few yards of the front door of Street Farm, Earl Soham, home of surgeon William Godwin. The good doctor kept meticulous details of these contraband convoys in his journal. Godwin must have known George Cullum, head of the Brandeston smugglers, and members of his gang.

The Queen, set well back from the road within its own large grounds, would have been an important customer of the free

The thatched single-storey 'Queen's Head' as the smugglers would have known it.

traders and the perfect place to provide victuals for fatigued men and fodder for tired horses.

Early in the afternoon of Sunday 16 May, 1784, a seizure of 57 half-ankers of spirits was made in the peaceful village of Kettleborough half-a-mile north of the pub. The Preventive force consisted of two supervisors named Bell and Pope, three Excise Officers named Engall, Mason and Spilling plus seven assistants. The following graphic account of the event subsequently appeared in the *Ipswich Journal* on 22 May:

> *'Sunday last, about two o'clock in the afternoon, a seizure of 57 half ankers of run spirits was made at Kettleburgh in this county, by Messrs. Bell and Pope, supervisors, and Messrs. Engall, Mason, and Spilling, excise-officers, with seven assistants. The same day, about four in the afternoon, as they were conveying these goods to Woodbridge, they were overtaken,*

near Easton, by a gang of villains, about 30 in number (all apparently stripped to their shirts, except one), who, with horrid imprecations, and expressions of Murder! Murder! fell upon them in a most unhuman manner, with an intent to rescue the seizure; however, the officers made a noble stand, and a bloody engagement ensued, which lasted near an hour, when the officers put the smugglers to flight, pursued them several miles, and maintained the seizure. Almost all the smugglers were wounded, and many of them were desperately, five or six of the officers' party were also slightly wounded. The officers and their assistants were armed with carbines, pistols, and broadswords – It is supposed the noted George Cullum, of Brandeston, was at the head of this banditti.'

Lillie, Alexander, Sophie and Maddie are part of the enthusiastic friendly team.

This former old farm house has a new look and feel in keeping with modern pubs. The youthful hosts, Alexander Aitchison and Lillie Fulford, took over in July 2015. Alexander is the chef while Lillie runs the front of house assisted by their young enthusiastic team.

The pub achieves the perfect mix of modernity in a traditional setting.

97

This lovely old settle is a charming feature in the traditionally furnished dining room.

The emphasis at The Queen is on fine dining.

One of Alexander's previous jobs was Chef de Partie in Cafe St Honore in Edinburgh. He brings many of the skills he learnt there to The Queen including baking his own bread daily. Alexander's venison, beetroot, carrot and sorrel makes an interesting starter; which can be followed by lamb with salsify, onions, mushrooms and leeks; and lastly for desert – lemon, honey and almond meringue.

The menu is built around locally sourced ingredients and Alexander and Lillie have plans to grow their own fruit and vegetables on land behind the pub. The aim is that vegetables will go from plot to pot in thirty minutes. There is also an interesting reasonably priced wine list and a changing selection of ales including representations from Adnams, Woodfordes, Timothy Taylor and Brakspear.

The pub was formerly known as 'The Queen's Head' and displayed in the bar is a newspaper article describing the devastating thatched roof fire that occurred on 3 August, 1958.

The changing selection of ales includes representations from Adnams, Woodfordes, Timothy Taylor and Brakspear.

A record of the devastating thatched roof fire that occurred on 3 August, 1958.

The pretty White Horse pub stands adjacent to Easton's small village green.

Easton
The White Horse

The Street, Easton, Woodbridge. IP13 0ED

Tel: 01728 746456

www.thewhitehorseeaston.com

Easton village nestles in the gentle valley of the River Deben 4 miles southeast of Earl Soham. The main street lies north of the river which bends in a loop quite close to the centre of the village before flowing away through acres of water meadows on either side.

Mentioned in the Domesday Book, the village was linked to the manor of Martley until 1627, when Sir Arthur Wingfield made the 150 acre estate his home. In 1688 Easton was purchased by the Prince of Orange for the Earl of Rochford. The fifth Earl introduced many improvements before he died in 1830 including surrounding the Easton Estate and house with its famous 'crinkle-crankle wall'.

The interior exudes style throughout the three smartly similar rooms.

On the death of the fifth Earl, the estate passed to the Duke of Hamilton, who rarely lived here, leaving the affairs in the hands of an agent who resided in the seventeenth-century Agent's House next to The White Horse Inn.

An interesting sequel to events that occurred a mile from The White Horse at Easton, on 16 May 1784 was revealed in the *Ipswich Journal* which appeared on 5 June. The owner of one of the horses used by the smugglers and captured by the Excise Men placed the following advertisement:

> 'WHEREAS a Black Mare, about 15 hands high, with a white mark on her nose, and one white leg behind, was on or about the 16th day of May last, taken on the road leading from EASTON toward KETTLEBOROUGH, by a party of excise officers, namely POPE, BELL, INGALL, MASON, SPELLING and CARTWRIGHT, or one of them, under

pretense of her belonging to me JOHN CAGE of HAWLEY in the County of Suffolk, now I, the said John Cage, as soon as can be discovered in whose possession the said mare is, intending to commence an action at law for the recovery thereof, do hereby offer a reward of Five guineas to any person detaining the said mare, and who will attend and give evidence of such person having the said mare, on the trial of such action in his possession.

JOHN CAGE
Hawley, June 5, 1784'

Open screens of ancient oak timbers help create a cosy intimate atmosphere.

It might be assumed that Cage was a member of the gang and was attempting to divert suspicion from himself but the Excise Officers were equal to this ploy. The Preventives placed their own advertisement in the paper on 23 June revealing the whereabouts of the mare:

Far removed from the original smugglers' pub interior the clever use of brick, flagstones and flint conveys a feeling of antiquity. *Below:* Although primarily functioning as a restaurant just calling in for a drink is also welcome.

'WHEREAS, JOHN CAGE, OF Haughley, in the county of Suffolk, did on the 5th inst., advertise a reward of Five Guiness to any person who would discover in whose custody a black mare was, which he insinuates to be his property and said to be taken, under a pretence of belonging to a gang of smugglers, near Easton, in this county, on 16th May last:

NOW THIS IS TO INFORM the said Cage. That a black mare taken that day is in the possession of Mr. Geo. W. Cartwright, of the Excise office , london, and if he, the said Cage, or any of his vile associates, will discover who it was that rode the said mare at that time , or any more or two of that gang of banditti, who attempted to murder the revenue officers, and to rescue the run goods then seized in their possession, he or they shall, on conviction of such persons, receive the sum of One Hundred pounds, to be paid by us or either of us.

The White Horse offers a choice of ten wines by the glass.

JOHN POPE
CHR. BELL
Supervisors
WM. ENGALL
WM. MASON
GEO. SPELLING
Officers of Excise'

Standing back from the small village green at Easton The White Horse is late sixteenth century with a nineteenth century plastered façade hiding the earlier timber framing. The original thatched roof now has pantiles to the rear and plain tiles at the front inset with two fairy-tale gabled dormer windows.

The central door, sheltered by a rustic timber porch, leads into a deceptively spacious interior divided into three smartly similar rooms. Farmhouse tables, country kitchen chairs, pews, settles and open fires all contribute to the simple elegant style.

The food philosophy is produce-dominated with good locally sourced ingredients 'from the sea', 'from the land' or 'from the field'. The menu choice is broadened with daily blackboard specials all designed to please walkers, diners and their children: with small portions of ricotta and aubergine cannelloni with arrabiata sauce, beer-battered haddock with hand-cut chips, crispy Dingley Dell pork belly with perfect mash and pearl barley, and an Earl Grey panna cotta. Beers are from Adnams with two local guest ales plus a choice of ten wines by the glass.

On winter evenings dogs doze in front of the log fires while platefuls of delicious food are ferried to plain wooden dining tables. In summer patrons can enjoy the partly walled garden screened by huge specimen trees from the old estate.

Beers are from Adnams with two local guest ales plus a choice of ten wines by the glass.

The Crown at Snape was standing here near the River Alde for a century before Shakespeare was born.

Snape
The Crown Inn
Bridge Road, Snape, Suffolk IP17 1SL
Tel: 01728 688324
www.snape-crown.co.uk

The small village of Snape lies on the River Alde close to Aldeburgh. It is best known today for its associations with composer Benjamin Britten, but throughout the nineteenth century its bridge was its most salient feature. This spot marked the navigable head of the River Alde and the first point at which it could be crossed without a boat.

Smugglers used the bridge to move contraband goods across the river, waiting first to see a light in a dormer window in the roof of The Crown. This signalled the all clear to smugglers and indicated the Militia stationed to guard the bridge were drinking in the bar below. The Crown also had a small windowless room accessed by a trap door through which casks and packages were hauled for temporary storage.

Unlike the Dragoons, the Militia was composed of non-professional soldiers. They were initially a 'Home Guard' formed to combat the threat of invasion during the Napoleonic Wars. Their officers were members of the local nobility who were often customers of the smugglers. The men themselves were mainly farm and estate workers many of whom would have had smuggling connections.

Snape was the scene of at least one unfortunate clash between free traders and the Preventives. In 1727, Excise Officer

The public area threads along beneath vast old beams and across mellow brick floors.

Landlady Teresa painted the dining room mural with her artist sister Maria.
Below: A cosy inglenook corner is created by the encircling arms of a huge double settle.

Jeremiah Gardiner came across a gang of smugglers near to Snape, misguidedly challenging the desperate men, despite being heavily outnumbered.

The aggrieved free traders replied with a volley of stones whereupon the brave officer drew his sword but the smugglers retaliated with cudgels. In the

The rosettes in the bar were awarded for the pub's own Gloucester Old Spot pigs.

fracas Gardiner's assailants overpowered him, cut off his nose with his own sword and left him lying in the road. While the free traders were otherwise engaged he managed to crawl off and hide behind a hedge. When one of the smugglers returned, doubtless with the intention of finishing him off, Gardiner heard the frustrated villain shout: *'Damn him, he's gone'*.

Getting on for 600 years old, this Adnams-owned village pub shelters beneath a most extraordinary saltbox pantile roof. Inside, the public area threads along beneath vast old beams and across mellow brick floors to cosy corners and an inglenook enclosed by the arms of a huge double settle. Part of the pub's 5 acres of land includes a spacious beer garden, ideal for summer dining.

An officer of the local Militia who were detailed to prevent smugglers crossing Snape Bridge.

On land behind The Crown, landlords Teresa Golder and Garry Cook run their own livestock smallholding with cattle,

Part of the pub's 5 acres of land provides a beer garden ideal for summer drinking and dining.

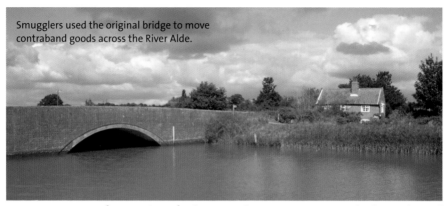

Smugglers used the original bridge to move contraband goods across the River Alde.

sheep, pigs, chickens, turkeys, goats, geese, ducks and quail while growing fruit and vegetables, ensuring a very local supply chain. They also support local suppliers of quality produce. Five minutes walk from Snape Maltings the pub offers pre- and post-concert dining but booking is advisable.

Smugglers looked for an 'all clear' light from a dormer window in the extraordinary saltbox pantile roof of The Crown.

Teresa who also goes fishing off Southwold for sea bass painted the pub's superb dining room mural together with her artist sister Maria. The fresco presents the story of Snape including the Maltings, the River Alde, the smugglers' bridge and The Crown's own small-holding farm.

Garry and Teresa took over The Crown in 2007. They have previous farming experience and are both chefs. Menus change frequently, but a sample features ham hock and leek, macaroni cheese, pheasant Wellington with truffle sauce and sirloin beef steak with field mushrooms, vine tomatoes, onion rings and chips. The food is complemented by Adnams beers and a choice of over thirty different wines.

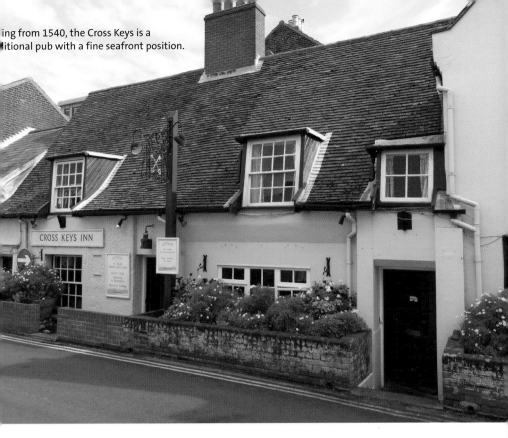

ing from 1540, the Cross Keys is a
litional pub with a fine seafront position.

CROSS KEYS INN

Aldeburgh
Cross Keys Inn
Crabbe Street, Aldeburgh IP15 5BN
Tel: 01728 452637

Aldeburgh today is peaceful and as different as can be
imagined from the dark days of smuggling. Now
second homes are the norm in this charming seaside
resort where candy-pink and powder-blue cottages
proliferate and fish and chip shops are outnumbered
by chichi boutiques and galleries. All one is likely to
encounter on the beach today is the odd fisherman and
a scattering of small boats but during the eighteenth
century things were very different. Lord Orford

remarked that the clergy, lawyers and doctors of the area were all smugglers and in Aldeburgh itself every inhabitant was one except the parson.

Early on a Sunday morning in April 1748 Customs Officers patrolling the beach near Aldeburgh found over 4 tons of tea and *'four small casks of liquor'* partially buried in shingle. Obviously it had been hidden until such time as the smugglers could transport it inland to one of the many places of concealment – a cottage, farmhouse, barn, inn or church.

A big wood-burning stove in the large inglenook is tucked in among comfortable pews and banquettes.

Thirty years later, in 1779, Lord Orford's Norfolk regiment camped at Aldeburgh, sent a party 4 miles up the coast to Sizewell on the news that a cutter was landing goods there. They arrived too late to intercept the landing, but found thirty half-ankers of spirits cleverly hidden away in a cave by the sea. A party was left camped on the spot to prevent more landings.

A little later a landing was made at Dunwich, 4 miles down the coast, and twenty militiamen mounted on baggage horses chased the smugglers 40 miles in four hours (presumably to Hadleigh). They failed to catch them but one smuggler had to abandon his load, which included a letter giving details of the next run. Again a detachment was sent to camp at the predicted landing point, where a cutter was seen hovering waiting its chance.

Adnams Southwold, Broadside and Ghost Ship are on handpump.

Fishermen still operate from the beach within sight of the pub.

In warm weather seats on the sheltered terrace with views across the promenad and shingle are quickly snapped up.

On 7 July 1880, whilst staying at The White Lion at the northern end of Aldeburgh beach, writer Edward Fitzgerald included the following reminiscences in a letter to his friend Charles Keene:

'I have, like you, always have, and from a Child had, a mysterious feeling about that "Sizewell Gap." There were reports of kegs of Hollands found under the Altar Cloth of Theberton Church nearby: and we Children looked with awe on the 'Revenue Cutters' which passed Aldbro', especially remembering one that went down with all hands, "The Ranger".'

The picturesque Old Custom House is situated towards the southern end of the High Street alongside candy-pink and powder-blue cottages.

Where most pubs have a beer garden the authentic sixteenth-century Cross Keys has a beach, and pints are seldom more pleasant than those sipped on the sea wall. Coiled ropes and lobster pots are piled between fishing boats, which rest at

The pub sources much of its marine menu from all of 20 yards away.

The old Aldeburgh Beach Lookout Tower welcomes a new artist in residence each week. *Above right:* On 7 July 1880, Edward Fitzgerald stayed at the White Lion and included boyhood reminiscences of local smuggling in a letter to a friend.

Early on a Sunday morning in April 1748 Customs Officers found over four tons of tea and 'four small casks of liquor' partially buried here in the shingle.

jaunty angles on the shingle, and the catch of the day is sold from wooden huts.

Dating from 1540, the Cross Keys is a traditional pub with a cheery bustling atmosphere. The interconnecting bars have antique and other pubby furniture and a wood-burning stove takes centre stage among comfortable pews and banquettes. The low ceilings are painted a warm orange and miscellaneous paintings hang on the mustard coloured walls.

The pub sources much of its marine menu from a supplier all of 20 yards away along the beach. Selections include the freshest halibut, skate wings, Dover sole, devilled whitebait, pints of prawns and Aldeburgh fish pie served with freshly made tartare sauce. Adnams Southwold, Broadside and Ghost Ship are on handpump, while decent wines by the glass and several malt whiskies are always available.

Orford
The King's Head
Front Street, Orford IP12 2LW
Tel: 01394 450271
www.thekingsheadorford.co.uk

Travelling east from either Wickham Market or Woodbridge, one discovers Orford at the very end of the road. Today this quintessentially English village attracts visitors who appreciate its tranquillity and enjoy its unrivalled landscape for walking, boating and bird watching.

Opposite the small quay, projecting into the River Alde, is Orford Ness, one of England's great natural curiosities. The 'Ness' is part of the long shingle bar which, over centuries, has been built up by the river's flow. As a result of the shifting, silting action, the Alde now enters the sea 11 miles from its original mouth cutting off Orford from the grey North Sea.

It was the building of the castle by Henry II that established Orford as an important centre, and led to the building of the

The King's Head occupies a commanding site in the heart of the village immediately in front of St Bartholomew's church whose tower is a centuries-old landmark for sailors.

church. As vessels became larger, the gradual denial of easy access to the sea created difficult fishing and trading conditions. By 1673 Orford was described as '*in former times a Town of good account for fishing, but that trade being lost, the Town cannot find itself*'. The hearth tax returns of the following year record five empty properties, 20 households too poor to pay the tax and only 37 households able to pay. Daniel Defoe described Orford in 1722 as '*once a good Town, but now decayed*'.

The circumstances that conspired against Orford's legitimate trade created a quiet haven with ideal conditions for the poor to embrace the illegal 'free trade'. This is confirmed by the following report which appeared in *The Ipswich Journal* on 28 February 1784:

The interior returns of the small first floor 'smugglers' window' are chamfered to direct the maximum amount of light from a lantern or candle in the direction of the river bank.

'*On the 30th ult., a seizure of 160 half ankers of gin, &c., was made at Orford, being part of the cargo of a smuggling cutter that bulged near that place; upon which the smugglers rescued their goods, and in the scuffle two of the officers were much*

The underside of the main beam in the dining room is fluted and the detail of rafter jointing is superior to general cottage architecture.

The roughhewn beams in the bar area are suggestive of salvaged ships' timbers. Both former cottage rooms are heated by wood-burning stoves. *Below:* Relatively new to the Adnams' range, Cashmere IPA is described as an American-style session IPA (at 4.7% abv) with a clean, smooth bitterness and fruity aromas of lemon, gooseberry and coconut.

The cellar is an architectural historian's delight with traces of old steps formerly leading to adjacent cottages, bricked up areas in the walls suggestive of tunnel entrances and extremely antiquated maritime timbers.

wounded. After the smugglers were gone, the officers made another seizure of goods out of the cutter, lodged them in a house in that town, and sent to Saxmundham for a party of dragoons, but about twelve at night a gang of about 30 smugglers, all armed, broke into the house where the goods were lodged and carried them off in triumph.'

Other villages and towns along the meandering Alde all saw their fair share of the free trade: Sudbourne, 2 miles north of Orford, was the home of a particularly notorious smuggler called Richard Chaplin. On his retirement Chaplin placed the following brazen advertisement in a local paper obviously calculated to cock-a-snook at the Revenue Men:

'Richard Chaplin, Sudbourne, Suffolk, near Orford, begs to acquaint his friends and the public in general That he has some time back declined the branch of smuggling and returns thanks for all their past favours.'

He goes on to list a whole range of items for sale including:

'A very useful Cart fit for a maltster, ashman or smuggler — it will carry 80 half ankers or tubs — one small ditto that will carry 40 tubs... and many articles that are useful to a smuggler.'

The remoteness of Orford made it a valuable spot for clandestine activities. Contraband landed at Hollesley Bay was run up the River Oare to be stored in The King's Head before being moved inland. The pub occupies a commanding site in the heart of the village immediately in front of St Bartholomew's church whose landmark tower has guided sailors into the safety of Orford for centuries.

The King's Head bar and adjoining dining room were formerly interiors of two different cottages, parts of which date from the thirteenth century. The fluted underside of the main beam in the dining room and the detail of rafter jointing is grander than general cottage architecture, suggesting this part of the building had ecclesiastical connections. The interior returns of the small first floor 'smugglers' window' are purposefully chamfered to direct the maximum amount of light from a signal lantern or candle.

The cellar is an architectural historian's delight with traces of old steps formerly leading to adjacent cottages, bricked up areas suggestive of tunnel entrances and extremely anti-

Orford's fortunes changed dramatically when King Henry II chose Orford as the site on which to build a new castle. Work began in 1165 and was completed in 1173.

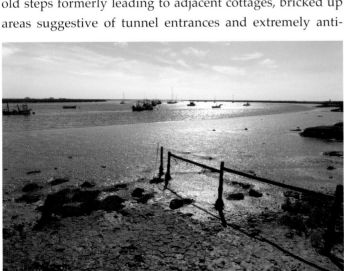

Orford Ness, forming the eastern bank of the river, is one of England's great natural curiosities.

121

The castle and church tower have been sailors' landmarks for centuries.

quated maritime timbers. If pub walls could speak it would be wonderful to have a conversation with The King's Head, hoping in particular the cellar would give up its secrets. When was it excavated? Who built the walls? Were there tunnels to the church and to the castle?

The menu includes a variety of pub lunch favourites and an evening selection incorporating modern British cuisine with twists on popular classics and an array of specials prepared from local, fresh, ingredients. The traditional Adnams' range of ales is complemented here by the newer Cashmere IPA plus a full and varied wine list.

Below left: The Old Customs House is a reminder of Orford's smuggling era.
Below right: The Coastguard Watch House still overlooks the old quay.

Shottisham
Sorrel Horse

The Street, Shottisham, IP12 3HD

Tel: 01394 411617

www.thesorrelhorse-shottisham.co.uk

'We believe the real pub is in danger but we must first attempt to define what we mean by a real pub. Providing a definition is not easy anymore than defining a great work of art is easy but, as with a great work of art, one knows when one is in the presence of the real thing.'

John Booth, *The Real Pub Guide*

Some of the local community folk who now own shares in the pub. The wonderful horse is from The Suffolk Punch Trust at Hollesley who are dedicated to preserving the breed and the skills of those needed to handle them.

Shottisham is located on the Bawdsey Peninsula and lies about 5 miles southeast of Woodbridge and around 3 miles

The homely cottage-style dining room.

Pub games are an integral feature of the traditional bar.

inland from the contraband coast at Hollesley Bay. Shingle Street, on the shore of the bay, is one of the most windswept and isolated communities in Suffolk. Remaining legacies of the free trade era are the row of Coastguard cottages and the old Martello Tower; one of the chain of small defensive forts built around the coast during the time of the threat of invasion from Napoleon's army.

The village street at Shottisham overlooks a slight hollow of meads and copses at the road crossing of Shottisham Creek, a tributary brook of the River Deben. The whole area here-abouts was a hotbed of smuggling.

One free trade story involves two Excise Officers, a father and son, named Cross who on Sunday, 12 September 1784, assisted by a party of the 1st Regiment of Dragoons, seized over 250 gallons of brandy and Geneva at Alderton, 2 miles south of Shottisham.

Alderton Hall had a tunnel leading from the inner hall, via St Andrew's church, to The Swan Inn at Alderton. This may originally have been a secret route for monks and a hiding place for Catholics during the Reformation but it seems likely local smugglers in the eighteenth century would have made good use of it. Goods, seized at Alderton were carried through lanes past the Sorrel Horse and successfully on to the Excise Office at Woodbridge.

Two decades later things were much the same. On Wednesday 10 October 1804 Riding Officer John Rogers who was stationed at Hollesley, experienced a rare rewarding day. The life of a Riding Officer was lonely and mainly frustrating. By the very nature of his calling, he could not have been blessed with many friends around Shottisham.

Adnams ales are drawn straight from the cask.

Rogers came to know a good deal about the cunning of local smugglers and their methods for concealing the results of their runs. Patrolling near the Sorrel Horse on this day he was looking keenly about him when he spotted something in a ditch which aroused his curiosity. Dismounting he was delighted to discover 140 tubs of Geneva.

Troops from the 1st Regiment of Dragoon Guards, mounted on Sorrel horses were called upon to assist local Preventive Men in combating smuggling.

From first glance this charming thatched sixteenth-century local holds out a great deal of promise and the interior does not disappoint. The Sorrel Horse has everything one might wish for in a village local although increasingly difficult to find.

The small-beamed room on the left, now used for dining, is heated with a wood burner with simple country-style chairs and pine tables standing on the wooden floor. The entrance door and the old dado wall panelling are painted in a warm magenta.

To the right, the public bar has a black and red quarry tiled floor. Beer is drawn on tap from casks behind the small 1950s' bar counter. There is a good log fire and games area with bar billiards and a 'Norfolk twister' gambling game on the beamed ceiling. For warmer weather there are tables on the sloping front lawn and in the small rear garden.

A wide range of freshly prepared seasonal dishes form the core of the menu, and a blackboard presents daily specials of starters, mains and desserts. The pub has a policy of supporting East Anglian breweries and the roster of beer includes; Adnams, Aspalls, Calvors, Cliff Quay, Earl Soham and Woodfordes.

A recent review by CAMRA (The Campaign for Real Ale) suggests an estimated 18 pubs are closing every week. When villagers from Shottisham and other folk from the surrounding area suspected their pub might close they took the initiative to acquire it for the community. After initial meetings in April and May 2011, they approached the owner, offering £350,000 which was accepted. An off-the-shelf company was created with five directors who raised the capital by selling shares in the business.

By August 2011 the group had 135 investors and enough cash to buy the pub. Subsequently they continued to raise an additional £100,000 for taxes, rethatching and other costs. The number of investors has now risen to 200 with most coming from local communities but some from as far away as Oman and Australia. Today the board of directors oversees the running of the pub which employs a full-time manager, two chefs and three attentive part-time bar staff.

The name 'Sorrel' refers to a copper-red shade of chestnut which is thought to originate from the colour of the flower spike of the sorrel herb. It is one of the most common equine coat colours.

The row of white Coastguard cottages stands back from the windswept beach at Shingle Street. To the far left is the low profile of the old Martello Tower.

SELECTED BIBLIOGRAPHY

Stan Jarvis: *Smuggling in East Anglia 1700 – 1840*
Richard Platt: *Smugglers' Britain*
Leonard P. Thompson: *Smuggling on the Suffolk Coast*

Terry Townsend's other Halsgrove titles include:

Once upon a Pint – A Readers' Guide to the Literary Pubs & Inns of Dorset & Somerset

East Cornwall Smugglers' Pubs – Kingsand to Mevagissey
West Cornwall Smugglers' Pubs – St Ives to Falmouth
Dorset Smugglers' Pubs
Hampshire Smugglers' Pubs
Isle of Wight Smugglers' Pubs
Kent Smugglers' Pubs

Jane Austen & Bath,
Jane Austen's Hampshire,
Jane Austen's Kent

Bristol & Clifton Slave Trade Trails